HOUSEBREAKING and TRAINING
YOUR NEW PUPPY

MICHAEL KELLY

CONTENTS

Photos by Tom Caravagia, Isabelle Francais, Celeste Meade, Louise van der Meid, Susan Miller, Robert Pearcy, R. Reagan, Vince Serbin, Sally AnneThompson.

Inside front cover: Rottweilers owned by Deborah Gilman. Photo by Isabelle Francais.
Inside back cover: Basenji photographed by Robert Smith.

THE BASICS

The basic, primary goal of housebreaking is to educate the dog as to the proper, desired place at which to relieve itself. The basic strategy by which housebreaking is achieved relies on consistency and praise. The owner's consistency begins with feeding the dog well and feeding it at regularly scheduled times. Consistency in feeding, especially with regard to the puppy, also applies to the constituents of each meal: the puppy's digestive system fares poorly against a haphazardly changing diet, which inevitably leads to houscbreaking set-backs. In all, the importance of feeding to the housebreaking procedure cannot be overstated, and thus the reader will find a chapter dedicated to proper feeding.

Consistency continues from feeding to include regular outings and exercise to provide adequate opportunities for the dog to relieve itself. It must be noted that the regularity and consistency required in both feedings and outings are not independent, but rather are interdependent. In other words, the two are closely related in that feedings trigger outings.

Very importantly, consistency follows through in praise and correction, the two basic tools that the owner uses to shape and train his dog. Praise, warm and lavish, should be given at each appropriate time, whenever the puppy successfully accomplishes a given task, even if it is with the owner's assistance. By giving praise, the dog is quickly brought to understand the desired behavior, and, through praise, the human-to-animal bond is strengthened. Correction takes the same basic shape as praise, for it too should be given at every appropriate time, whenever the puppy performs an act which is undesirable. Correction, like praise, must be given at the time of the action.

that is accomplished without effort. While this book provides the most direct, tried-and-true methods of housebreaking, and highlights the time-costly mistakes to avoid, it will be demonstrated that time is of the essence, for truly it is consistent daily time spent with the new dog that provides the housebreaking chemical within every housebreaking prescription.

Puppies have a mind of their own. Yet, with appropriate praise and correction, most puppies can be brought to the desired level of training. Basset Hounds.

Praise (reward) or correction, when given some time after the action, will fail to have its desired effect, namely reinforcement or deterrence of the act. This fact is vitally important for the housebreaker to keep in mind. Far too often are dogs, especially young puppies, corrected for an action that they performed in the owner's absence. The owner returns to find a soiled environment and scolds the dog. It is not of the ability of most dogs, especially young ones, to associate the correction with the past action. More likely, the puppy will associate the correction with his happiness of his owner's arrival.

The instrumentality of praise and correction, and their need to accompany the proper or improper action, brings us to another very important housebreaking factor—that of the owner's time. Housebreaking is not something

HOUSEBREAKING AND BEYOND

A properly housebroken dog is the desire of every owner, if for no other reason than an unhousebroken animal is an impossible home companion. Yet, housebreaking, housebreaking properly, extends far beyond the mere immediate ends to which the process is geared. Housebreaking has been called the foundation upon which all future training is built, and there lies much truth and merit in this statement. Though the basic training commands such as sit, stay, and down, may be learned by the dog prior to his becoming completely housebroken, the housebreaking process is the first time in which owner and dog work together on an all-day, daily training routine: whereas training the dog to sit may require 15 minutes a day for several weeks, housebreaking demands a 24-hour-a-day schedule and constant, consistent communication between owner and animal. In addition to laying the foundation for all subsequent training, housebreaking also forms the base on which the owner-to-dog relationship will be constructed. It is therefore of utmost importance that the housebreaking process be approached and executed intelligently and properly.

The dog owner has a lot working in his favor, not the least of which is the dog's preference for cleanliness and inherent desire to please its master. Also to the owner's advantage is the bulk of research and written experience regarding the housebreaking process, which forms the basis for this book. Therefore, despite the importance that is attached to housebreaking, the owner should relax and view the upcoming weeks of training the dog as a rewarding process that is fully under his control, a process which, when completed, will provide the basic framework for the building of the ideal person-to-pet relationship.

HOUSEBREAKING DEFINED

As stated, housebreaking is the process by which the puppy learns where to relieve itself. It is a delicate process because the ramifications of the process can be many and distressing, if it is not conducted intelligently, with certain given, necessary factors

Beneath the obviously different colorations of these seven-week-old Akita littermates lie equally different personalities, which may not be as apparent at this early age as the dogs' physical characteristics. Owners, Bob and Nadine Fontano.

keen in the housebreaker's mind. Labeling housebreaking as delicate is not to frighten the new dog owner, for despite the possible repercussions of a faulty procedure, housebreaking is most assuredly bound to succeed when conducted according to one of the three basic methods proposed in this book. The three methods, crate training, paper training, and litterbox training, are each suited best to specific owner circumstances; and taken together they cover the broad range of possible new-dog owner situations and needs.

COMMON ERRORS

Common mistakes made by people when housebreaking their dog include: starting too early; not restricting the dog sufficiently; not spending enough time on housebreaking; expecting too much too soon; providing inconsistent praise and/or punishment; and not keeping the dog's environment clean.

Starting Early No dog, with very rare exceptions, has the physical ability to successfully complete the housebreaking procedure before it is three months of age, and few have this ability before they are four months of age. Starting the dog early on the road to housebrokeness is simply a bad idea, and yet many new dog owners impatiently attempt it.

Fortunately for us, we can learn from their mistakes. It is a common human belief that, if one tries hard enough, one will eventually succeed, and this philosophy seems inevitably to find itself being applied to the canine pet. Regardless of how applicable or non-applicable it is to human beings, this philosophy does not apply to the dog in housebreaking that is under the age of four months. The simple reason is that the dog does not possess the basic physical ability to control its bowels at this young age, and housebreaking before bowel and bladder control are achieved by the dog results only in *negative* results.

Starting early, with the notion that the dog will get *something* positive out of the experience, is another basis from which new-dog owners apply housebreaking procedures before the puppy is ready. It seems that this second notion is often applied in conjunction with the first, together resulting in a doomed housebreaking experience. We can conclude from the reports of owners who have applied the human-based concepts of "try and ye shall succeed" and "even failure brings learning and growth" that starting the puppy early on the road to housebroken happiness not only brings immediate failure but results in possibly insurmountable

6

set-backs for future training. Indeed, canine behaviorists have determined that the inevitable high-volume correction that accompanies premature training is detrimental to the future psychological development of the dog; additionally, this correction, whether in large quantities or small doses, when applied to behavior over which the dog has no physical control, can rob the canine of any sense of worth which it might be cultivating. These findings and conclusions are but a few of the more significant ones. Based on them, we can confidently say that housebreaking should not begin in earnest until the puppy reaches the appropriate age, namely the age at which it has control over its bladder sphincter muscles.

Poor Restriction Confining the housebreaking dog to a given, small location is vital to the successful housebreaking process. There are two common mistakes which the housebreaking owner can make in this aspect of the housebreaking procedure. The first applies to the time before the

An adorable eight-week-old Labrador Retriever from MiJan's Kennels. It is often at this age that puppies leave for their new homes with their permanent owners.

7

housebreaking process begins. Most puppies reach their new homes between the ages of two to three months, before housebreaking can begin. Unlike the actual housebreaking procedure, which focuses on the dog's elimination, restriction should be applied consistently

animal will sulk and whine, which will only complicate and add to the stress of housebreaking. It must be remembered that the puppy is used to a restricted area: prior to its arrival at your home, the puppy's world consisted of its box and a small surrounding area. While the young dog will likely enjoy the new-found freedom offered in its new home, it will not miss it during its early months if such freedom is not provided. Additionally, offering a large span of territory to the young pup in many cases will overwhelm it, adding to the stress and uncertainty of the puppy in its new, strange environment. By keeping the dog in a restricted area (ideally the same area that will form the confined housebreaking territory) from the time it enters

from the time the new puppy enters the home. The reason is that restriction plays a vital role once the process commences. If the pup is allowed free run of the house, or even a considerable portion of the house, it may come to see the housebreaking confinement as a sort of punishment, which it will not understand and will likely "resent" or "rebel against"; in many cases, the suddenly confined

your home is one very important step in achieving a successfully housebroken animal with minimal time and effort.

The second way that new-dog owners err in the housebreaking procedure is not restricting the dog sufficiently during the housebreaking procedure. Regardless of the method; whether crate, paper, or litter box; restricting the dog to a small area, especially when acute supervision is not available, is most important to quick housebreaking with minimal correction. The dog's living area should include no more than a few square yards of space, and this space may be further limited during the absence of proper supervision. The necessity of a restricted area is discussed in more detail in the chapters dealing with the specific methods of housebreaking, but suffice it to say here that properly confining the new puppy to a given living space from the time it enters its new home offers the best opportunity for successful, easy housebreaking.

Insufficient Time The importance of time to housebreaking, and indeed to the pet experience in general, must never be overlooked by any dog owner. Time comes in two packages, basic time and quality time, and both are extremely important to housebreaking. Each day of housebreaking, the dog owner will be required to spend several hours of basic time to oversee, feed, and clean-up after the dog. There is no limit (beyond the given number of hours in the day) to the amount of basic time which the owner can or should give to the dog. In addition to basic time, quality time must include at least an hour or two of each day. Quality time includes

play, walks, and the various ways in which humans and dogs communicate.

It seems apparent, from the letters received by this author and from the various published articles and texts on housebreaking and dog ownership, that too many new dog owners expect housebreaking to occur naturally, with little effort, and even less time spent on the process. It seems reasonable to place partial blame on some of the published material circulating in the dog world today. Emphasis, apparently too much emphasis, is given to the dog's inherent desire for a clean environment and its preference not to soil its immediate territory. While these factors are thankfully present in the domestic canine, their power to execute (even initiate) successful housebreaking are negligible without the consistent effort of the dog owner (a necessary qualifier missing from too many accounts of the dog's cleanliness instincts).

Not spending enough time on housebreaking, whether the result of misleading reports or shear

Early restriction is essential not only to successful housebreaking but also to other training procedures—not the least of which is conditioning the pup (or puppies) to keep off dad's easychair.

negligence, is perhaps the greatest shortcoming that one can apply to housebreaking. It seems that time, basic and quality, can compensate to a fair degree for any other mistake an owner can make along the housebreaking road. As a final note, we need again to emphasize the importance of housebreaking as a process whereby the foundation for future training and the future person-to-pet relationship is built. This foundation will be sound and solidly constructed only if the appropriate amount of time is given to the housebreaking process. Should the owner not provide the daily quality moments, should the owner slack in supervision, should the owner not clean up promptly, then housebreaking will be hindered, and most importantly, the base for the future will be shabby indeed.

Misunderstanding Although it sounds trite, a dog is not a human being. The young dog does not understand our spoken or our body language as yet; although it may one day soon come to grasp many of our verbal and physical communications, it will never fully comprehend the nuances of human expression. Thus, when after a new-dog owner takes careful time to demonstrate and explain desired behavior and the young pup responds quite to the contrary, scolding or other punishment should not be given—even frustration, likely understandable from the human point of view, does not belong in the housebreaking process in these instances. Yet, too often dog owners tend to look at their young dog as a comprehending though incorrigibly stubborn animal or, on the flip side of the coin, as an irreparably stupid being. Of course, neither of these perceptions are correct or even justified. They are merely the result of human ignorance of the canine. Thus, it is repeated that a dog is not a human being; the owner needs to understand and accept that the dog should be perceived as a dog, an intelligent animal that will learn its role and appropriate place in the human society only through the consistent application of the appropriate doses of praise and correction over a period of time, which traces clearly to the essential basics of housebreaking, namely patience, persistence, and praise.

Failed Conditioning
Housebreaking is no doubt a process of conditioning in the psychological sense of the word. In this sense, conditioning is a learning process whereby appropriate behavior (response) is taught by the receiving of punishment and praise (stimuli). To understand this clearly, a brief note on basic conditioning is

necessary. The two primary types of conditioning are classical and operant conditioning. Classical conditioning refers to the type of stimulus-response actions described by Ivan Petrovich Pavlov, as determined by his studies of the salivary reflex in dogs. In these studies, meat served as the unconditioned stimulus: when meat was placed in front of the dog, the salivary glands were activated. The activation of the salivary glands was the response. At the same time that the meat was provided, a bell was rung. The bell became the conditioned stimulus, for as time went on, the dog came to (was conditioned to) associate the bell with the meat. Pavlov found that, in time, the bell could be rung without providing meat and the dog's salivary glands would be activated; the bell thus became a conditioned stimulus.

Operant conditioning is based on the theory of the American psychologist Edward Lee Thorndike, who in his "Law of Effect" outlined the concept of learned behavior based on the response (or effect) which the environment provided to the behavior

(stimulus). According to the "Law of Effect," if the response to the stimulus is positive (pleasant) the behavior will be reinforced. If, however, the response is negative (something pleasant is removed) the behavior will be weakened. Considered the forerunner of operant conditioning, B.F. Skinner made great strides in the understanding of this aspect of learning and is considered the father of Behavioral Psychology.

In classical conditioning, it is the stimulus that is controlled. The response is reliant upon a previously existing condition or reflex. In operant conditioning, on the other hand, it is the response which can be controlled, and the stimulus (behavior) which is already present. By examining

Though unaware of behavioral theories, mother canines practice positive and negative reinforcement when shaping the behavior of their young offspring. Labrador Retrievers owned by Fran Opperisano, Joan Huebel, and Janet Farmilette.

11

these two types of conditioning, the dog owner can better understand the roles of praise and correction, as well as consistency, in the housebreaking process.

We have already touched on the pup's limited capacity to hold its excreta; it is known that in the young dog the pressure exerted on the bowels and bladder by a full stomach will necessitate the puppy's going out in about 15 to 30 minutes. Feeding, or creating the full stomach, is thus the classical stimulus; it is controlled by the owner. The classical response is the dog's need to go. Because we know that within 15 to 30 minutes after feeding the puppy will evacuate, we can watch closely for the right signs and then take the puppy out, or simply take the puppy out 10 to 15 minutes after feeding and wait with him outside until the inevitable action occurs. At this point, operant conditioning comes into play: while the puppy is relieving itself (operant stimulus) the owner should provide warm and lavish praise (response) to reinforce the behavior. In the same light, correction in the form of verbal reprimand should be given while the pup is in the act of soiling the home, thus weakening the action. Thus, the dog is conditioned to the goals of housebreaking classically by the owner's feeding and taking the dog outside according to a

strict schedule, and the dog is conditioned operantly by the appropriate use of praise and reprimand in accordance with the puppy's behavior.

Providing inconsistent praise and/or punishment is a frequent problem which canine trainers come across in talking with their clients. It seems, based on their reports, the correspondence of the author, and the published literature on the subject, that many owners complicate the dog-training procedure—housebreaking included but not exclusive—by praising some behavior some of the time and/or by correcting some behavior some of the time. At other times, these once-praised or corrected behaviors are let pass without response, or, worse yet, are responded to with a contradictory message. The most likely root cause of this owner behavior is an ill-defined set of training goals, and this extends well beyond house training. Insufficient and contradictory response to behavior has been found not only to affect negatively the behavior in question but also to affect negatively other behaviors which are conditioned, or to be conditioned, through praise and reprimand. It seems that poor response to behavior not only confuses the dog as to the appropriateness of the behavior but also to the meaning of the response. Nothing could be worse to the owner attempting to housebreak his dog than to have his dog come not to understand the nature of his praise and punishment, the housebreaker's two most basic, most instrumental tools. Thus, before embarking on the housebreaking route, clearly establish in your mind the goals that you wish to attain during the housebreaking process.

Not Keeping It Clean As briefly mentioned, dogs are innately clean animals, believably possessing the instinct not to soil their immediate environment. It was also stated that many owners overestimate the power of the innate cleanliness in dogs and rely too heavily upon it to serve as a vital housebreaking tool. It is true that the desire to be clean and the natural hesitancy of dogs to soil their environment are important and highly useful to the housebreaking procedure, but owners must keep in mind that they alone will not housebreak the dog. Additionally, these instincts are not as strong as some behaviorists have proposed, and if the owner is not careful, these instincts can be easily lost in the young dog: if the puppy, and to a lesser extent the adult dog, is forced to live for any prolonged period of time in a soiled environment, it may come to perceive the soiled environment as what is expected by the owner. In other words, the dog will see the soiled environment as the desire of the owner. Given time, the dog

All dogs have the potential to become uncontrollable animals. With this fact in mind, one can really appreciate the value of early conditioning when admiring this so well-behaved and massive a Mastiff owned by Winterwood Kennels.

13

will be conditioned to such surroundings and possibly even adapt its ways to keep its environment soiled. If the dog, especially the puppy, becomes conditioned to a soiled environment, it will be at the cost of weakening—or for all intents and purposes eliminating—the innate tendency for a clean environment, and the dog will be less likely to exert conscious control over its elimination; it will be less inclined towards the housebreaking procedure.

Given these findings, it is easy to see how owners who fail to maintain a consistently clean environment add considerable difficulty to the housebreaking process. Consistency is the key word in the preceding sentence; keeping the pup's environment clean for the majority of the time is not enough: though you are tired or simply don't feel like doing it, though you rationalize that it's not *that* dirty, clean the area anyway, or, if you must be absent for a period, have someone else stop by and clean the area. The author makes this adamant request not because a single dirty day will ruin the pup for life—puppies

are much more resilient than that—but because keeping the environment clean *all* of the time greatly facilitates the entire housebreaking procedure, making it a faster, more effective process.

SUMMING IT UP

With housebreaking defined, with its rules and restrictions covered, and with the most common owner mistakes discussed, we are ready to look closely at the three basic ways to housebreak a dog, namely crate training, paper training, and litterbox training. In each of these methods, the goals and rules, as well as the mistakes, already outlined equally apply. The housebreaking owner is encouraged to read each of the discussed methods in their entirety before selecting the one which he will employ. Each method has its advantages and its setbacks, but each is best suited to a specific owner–dog situation.

Dottidale Dalmatian pups at ten weeks of age. These two pups demonstrate two possible spot colorations of the breed: pup on the left, black; pup on the right, liver.

14

CRATE TRAINING

This rambunctious litter of Brittany puppies prepares for a trip to the vet in an all-wire canine carrier.

Crate training involves instilling routine into the young dog's life. Because all animals, including dogs, are creatures of habit, the housebreaking owner has the immediate advantage and is reinforced by the tools of the crate and conscious command of the instincts of the dog. Essentially, crate training involves utilizing the crate as a type of "home turf" for the dog, as well as a confining instrument which acts to limit the dog's possible areas of excretion. If employed thoughtfully and consistently, crate training may indeed be the quickest, surest, and easiest way to housebreak a dog.

Before we continue, a common hesitation of dog owners must be addressed: that confining a dog to a crate is cruel or harmful to the dog is certainly not true in the case of proper crate training. It is likely that many dog owners view the crate as detrimental to the dog's psychological development because of the fair resemblance of the crate to a small prison cell, which, of course, is our primary tool for social correction. This notion should be dismissed at the outset of the ensuing discussion: first because of the primary difference between man and dog, and second because the crate, when employed as directed, can actually add comfort and build confidence in the dog, without any of the negative effects associated with confinement or restriction of the human animal.

Many canine behaviorists assert that crate training is one of the best methods of housebreaking a dog. This assertion is based on the relative quickness of the completed process, the reduced degree of error (soiling the home both during and after the training), and the reduced need for correction and scolding throughout the housebreaking experience.

Crate training is not for everyone. It is best suited for owners of indoor dogs that are to be trained to do all of their elimination during walks and/or when let out to the yard. Of course, it is equally good for dogs who will spend their days outdoors and their nights indoors, but such dogs should spend the majority of their crate-training days indoors, being let out only for exercise and excretion. Crate training is definitely not for owners who do not have the time available on a regular daily basis to play and exercise with the young dog. Additionally, if the dog is to be solely an indoor dog and not be let

out except on infrequent occasions or even once a day, crate training is not the best housebreaking option; paper training or litterbox training becomes the method of choice in these instances.

With the dog owner's initial possible hesitation covered, and all the obviously outstanding benefits on the side of crate training, what could possibly deter the dog owner from opting for this method? There are two apparent drawbacks of the crate method of housebreaking: crate training demands initially more time and commitment from the owner than the long-established method of paper training, and crate training requires the initial purchase of the crate. At first glance these two drawbacks may seem to outweigh the aforementioned advantages of the procedure. However, after brief consideration, the all-important time and money become dividend-reaping investments. First, regarding time, crate training usually involves a sum total of an extra hour per day over that required for paper training. The bulk of crate training usually requires four weeks to complete, whereas the same degree of completeness in paper training usually requires five to six weeks. Thus, while crate training "costs" roughly seven hours a week extra, it saves one to two full weeks of paper changing, deodorizing, and worry. Our second drawback, purchasing the crate, is similarly nullified when we consider the practical necessity of owning a crate. If the owner is considering any degree of travel with his dog, then a crate becomes almost standard equipment. Traveling with a dog without a proper crate is downright dangerous. Additionally, the few hotels and motels which accept pets invariably require that they be kept in just such a crate while in the room. Even if you are not considering extensive travel, the requisite trips to the vet, the park, and other occasional outings should entail the use of a crate, for otherwise you are assuming unwarranted risk of injury to your charge and indeed yourself—the number of automobile accidents caused by unrestrained dogs is well documented.

THE CRATE

The best crate for housebreaking is made of sturdy plastic. It should have a front door that ideally is of coated sturdy wire to enhance ventilation and offer a view when latched closed. Ventilation is very important to the comfort and security of the dog, so be sure that the crate allows air passage through at least two of its sides.

Unless your breed is a particularly small one, you will probably have to purchase two crates during the course of responsible dog ownership: you will need one crate sized appropriately for the puppy and a second, later one sized correctly for the adult dog. Accept this fact as inevitable, and do not buy a crate which is too large for the young dog with the idea that he will grow into it. A crate which is

These four-week-old Australian Shepherds are surely too young to begin housebreaking, but they not too young to start their crate-acclimatization experience. Owner, Joseph Hartnagle.

too large is one that provides enough room for the dog to sleep comfortably after he has soiled the other half. In a crate of this size, the dog can claim as *his* territory the clean area of the crate, while likely happily making the far side a permanent dumping ground. Obviously, if this behavior occurs, house-breaking can be seriously hindered. Additionally, a crate of this size is not safe for car travel because the roominess of the crate will allow the dog to be thrown about in the event of an accident.

For best housebreaking results, the dog should be introduced to the crate before beginning the actual housebreaking process.

Though this is not necessary, early introduction generates the best possible setting for housebreaking by having the dog already acclimated to the crate. Ideally, if the crate is properly introduced to the pup or dog, the animal will be more than acclimated (actually fond of) the crate.

In many cases, the dog's first experience with the crate will be its journey home with its new owner. Because this experience often involves the young pup's most extensive-to-date auto journey, which is necessarily traumatic, it may be best to acclimate the pup even before bringing him home. Most

responsible dog breeders are very cooperative and will gladly work with the new owner within reason. If you wish to have the breeder initiate the crate, ask him to follow roughly the ideas presented in this next paragraph.

Place the crate in a warm, dry, comfortable location, away from foreign noises, drafts, and distractions. Importantly, when first introducing the crate, have it located in a room temporarily free of other animals, especially fellow competitive dogs. Have the crate positioned, and assembled with any extras desired, before introducing the pup. Possible supplements can include the pup's favorite blanket or toy placed in or near the crate and a safe chew product to occupy the dog pleasantly and constructively after it makes its new home of the crate. With the crate so established, introduce the puppy to its crate as the puppy's own. This is accomplished by talking to the puppy in the same manner as when instructing (not commanding or correcting) him to any other object, e.g., "Here Billy, this is your crate; see, isn't it nice." Let the pup look, sniff and explore with all its senses. Of course, the puppy must assuredly not be allowed to urinate or defecate in or near the crate during this early introduction period.

Many owners are surprised when the pup wanders right into the crate and retires for a nap. As mentioned, the crate can afford an increased sense of security to the young animal by providing him with a sound place to claim as his territory, a place enclosed as in the dens of historical dog. Inevitably though, some dogs will not take so easily and quickly to the crate. Some will act indifferently, not really sure of its benefits or intentions, while a select few may even despise it. Not to fear, however, if your dog is the one who refuses to accept the crate, for the crate will still provide the vital function of canine carrier, which responsibly should be used even for initial transport home. For most dogs, however, all that is required is a little time, perhaps time enough to tucker-out and then select a napping place. Invariably for the majority of dogs, especially young puppies, the crate readily becomes their own; if they do not love it, they at least accept it well enough for its great utility in the housebreaking process. Though some experts may differ, it is the opinion of this author that if the dog for some reason absolutely abhors the crate (perhaps due to a terrible flight experience if the dog was transported by air previous to new ownership) then an alternative method, such as the well-tried paper training method, should be employed. Forcing the dog to be

"For best housebreaking results, the dog should be introduced to the crate before beginning the actual housebreaking process."

confined by an object which instills deep fear can elicit detrimental effects in the animal. Of course, hesitation or indifference to the crate is not the "deep fear" of which we speak.

Once all is well between dog and crate, and the crate is positioned in its permanent location (which in home introduction should ideally be the same as the location for initial

introduction), the contents of the crate can include a blanket, towel or other suitable bedding, a safe chew toy, and a few objects which you feel will make the pup more pleased with his new home. It is best not to clutter the crate but rather to let the pup perceive plenty of space in which to stretch out and claim as his own.

CRATE ACCLIMATION

It is best to let the puppy gradually become used to being locked in the crate during the day. If the pup associates the crate with a pleasant experience, it will feel more comfortable in it and will be more inclined to use it in the future. Of course, acclimating the puppy to the crate takes times, but like most other canine-training investments, the rewards are well worth the initial effort.

Fortunately, time is on the side of most new puppy owners: because no dog can be housebroken before it is three to six months of age, the dog owner typically has several weeks to fully acclimate the puppy to the crate before the housebreaking process begins in earnest.

The first day of acclimation (which can be the first day the puppy enters its new home) includes locking the puppy in the crate for about five minutes. The owner should stay in sight of the puppy for the entire time to add to the pup's security. After the given time has elapsed, the puppy should be let out of the crate and praised warmly; this will generate a pleasurable experience in association with staying in the crate. This five-minute stay can be repeated several times for the first day or so, taking caution not to overdo the experience. Depending on how well the puppy responds to its five-minute stay, the time spent in the crate should be regularly increased on a daily basis. Do not force the dog to stay too long in the crate if it is acutely uncomfortable, and at the same time do not be too weak or lenient by letting the dog out because it whimpers and whines. (As a tip, if the puppy is placed in the crate after play time, and of course after feeding and evacuation, it will likely be more inclined to settle down in its crate without protest and may not surprisingly take a little nap.) The time which the pup spends in the crate should be increased until it reaches one half-hour, always with the owner remaining within sight of the dog.

Once the half-hour is reached, the owner should drop the time back to five to ten minutes again, this time with his leaving the room. Likely the pup will whine for the owner's return, and it is important not to give in too quickly. In due time the puppy will settle down, and soon it will

"Inevitably though, some dogs will not take so easily and quickly to the crate."

believes that the puppy should *not* be allowed to sleep in the owner's bedroom, unless of course the owner intends to allow the dog to sleep in the room throughout its life.

Though the author cannot state which night-time placement is best for the reader, he can say that he sides more with the latter position than with the former. The basic reason for which is the fact that if the puppy is allowed to sleep in its master's room, it may well have a difficult time adjusting to sleeping elsewhere, which can make for many sleepless, trying nights. If these trials coincide with the housebreaking period, considerable stress and difficulty could be added to the process. The former position does have its merits, however, especially regarding the fact that the owner can more readily let the dog out if it needs to relieve itself during the night. But, if conducted properly, housebreaking should eliminate the night-time need rather quickly. Essentially, it is up to the housebreaking owner as to where the crate should be placed at night.

The owner of these Beagles utilizes two different types of canine crates, namely the all-wire and the sturdy plastic. This reminds us that, if your particular dog dislikes the more enclosed plastic crate, you might opt for the all-wire one, or vice

become quite comfortable in its familiar crate surroundings. This owner-absence time should also be increased gradually until it reaches one half-hour, at which time the dog should be fully acclimated to the crate and ready to spend the periods within it which are required for crate training.

There remains considerable debate regarding the placement of the crate during the night hours when the family retires. One school of thought believes that the puppy should be locked in its crate for the night and the crate should be located in the owner's bedroom, possibly beside the bed. People who adhere to this belief cite the added security that such placement affords the puppy, and also claim that, if the puppy whimpers because it needs to relieve itself, the owner can then take the puppy outdoors, thus facilitating the housebreaking procedure. There is also a school of thought which

THE PROCESS

When your dog is over four to

six months of age and properly acclimated to the crate, you are ready to begin crate training. With proper crate acclimation completed, crate training becomes a relatively simple procedure, the key to which is routine. A daily routine, or schedule, should be drawn up prior to commencing the crate-training process. It should include all important daily activities, including feeding, walks, exercise and play, crate time, etc. As an example, the housebreaking owner might draw up a schedule such as this:

6:30: awake; quick walk.

6:45: morning meal, while I clean the crate and area.

7:00: play time, while I get ready for work.

7:30: walk until pup goes (last walk before leaving).

8:00: lock pup in crate; leave for work.

12:00: return for lunch; quick walk, feed (while I straighten), play (while I eat), walk until goes (last walk before leaving).

12:45: return to work.

5:15: home from work; good walk; feed (while I straighten), play (while I eat), walk again.

6:00: quality time, some basic training, lots of love.

8:00: supervised play

9:00: biscuit or other treat; last water before bedtime.

9:30: quick walk.

11:00: long walk (last walk before bedtime).

11:30: in the crate for the night.

This list serves to illustrate the necessary routine required for successful crate training. It is demanding—perhaps too demanding for some—but the better the routine and the more closely it is followed, the quicker and more unwavering are the results. From the work hours apparent in the above schedule, it is obvious that it was drawn up for the working owner's weekday. Of course, not every dog will be housebroken by a working owner. If you, your husband or wife, or any other member of your household will be housebreaking the dog and does not have to work, then considerably more flexibility is given in the formation of a schedule. Nonetheless, it is most important that, whatever schedule is adopted, it be maintained from day to day. For working owners, it is important that the schedule not alter too much during the weekends, especially regarding feeding and walks. The owner can and should, of course, provide more hours of quality time, supervised play, and training during the weekend or whenever else time is available. The adopted schedule should be followed closely for the duration of the crate training procedure, which—if attempted with a physically ready, well-prepared puppy—should last

"There remains considerable debate regarding the placement of the crate during the night hours when the family retires."

about 20 to 30 days.

The reason that strict adherence to routine is essential in crate training is that dogs are creatures of habit. In truth, strict adherence to the schedule is more important than the basic schedule itself—the reason being that dog's are *highly adaptable* creatures of habit. This means that the dog will (within reason, of course) mold its ways to fit the given schedule. However, changing the schedule, once established, becomes difficult and trying to the habitual creature. By the same token, constantly changing the schedule never allows the habitual nature of the dog to be used effectively in the housebreaking procedure.

As an essential part of the schedule, the puppy must be allowed out of the crate frequently enough so that it can keep the crate (its home) clean. Puppies have a limited capacity for retaining their urine and excreta—typically no more than four hours, though proper feeding and watering at night time can extend the period to roughly eight hours. If the puppy is forced to soil its crate, especially if it is then forced to live with its excreta for several additional hours, due to the owner's absence, the crate training procedure suffers measurable setbacks. Repeatedly allowing (forcing) the dog to live with its waste can produce an unhousebreakable animal and likely an animal with acute behavior problems. Even with occasional prolonged absences which leave the puppy with its waste, it becomes likely that housebreaking will be made more difficult because the puppy becomes accustomed to living with its excrement. Crate training

relies rather heavily on the fact that puppies are less likely to soil their immediate environment, an instinct that grows stronger with age. The housebreaking owner must use this instinct to its fullest potential and not weaken it in any way by poor housekeeping or failure to adhere to the determined schedule established for the duration of the housebreaking process. It becomes tediously obvious at this point that crate training is not for every new dog owner but is best reserved for those who have the time and dedication required for this rather arduous, though rewarding, two-week task.

The crate itself should be permanently located in a contained area, which will prevent the puppy from wandering off to a far corner of the house to relieve itself. (As mentioned earlier, the crate can be moved to the housebreaker's bedroom for the night, if so desired.) Most owners locate the crate in a section of their kitchen, furnished basement, or playroom. The best surface on which to place the crate is one of linoleum or tile, one that is easy to clean should it get soiled. Many owners also line the area surrounding the crate with paper, which also facilitates clean-up should it be necessary. The enclosed area itself should be at least 4 x 6 feet; it can be larger but should not be so large as to allow

the dog to relieve itself some distance from the crate. Additionally, the enclosed area should contain some play things and a safe chew product, such as a Nylabone, Gumabone, or Chooz, to keep the dog occupied and to allow it to work off its doggie tensions. Because a 4 x 6 area is by no means large enough to provide the dog with sufficient exercise opportunity, regular outings and walks play a very important role in keeping the dog happy and fit.

When supervision is present, the door of the crate should be left open and the puppy should be free to enter and exit the crate. During supervision the owner must watch carefully for signs that the pup is going to urinate or defecate. At the first sign, the puppy should be quickly, gently picked up and taken to the chosen place of evacuation. The owner should stay with the dog until it does its business. Immediately following, even during, the pup's business, warm, lavish praise must be given. The puppy must come to know that it is doing good by going at the spot to which the owner brought it. After praise, the puppy can then be returned to its restricted area and allowed to play.

At all times when strict supervision is not possible, the puppy should be locked in the crate. However, the pup must be

"By the same token, constantly changing the schedule never allows the habitual nature of the dog to be used effectively in the housebreaking procedure."

A well-trained German Wirehaired Pointer and a proud young owner.

taken to the chosen area of evacuation regularly, as soon as the owner returns or morning arises. If the pup is left too long in the crate, it will not be able to hold in its excrement and will necessarily soil its crate. In this case a scolding should *not* be given. It is not the pup's fault, and besides the pup does not associate punishment with an action that occurred in the past.

The necessary regimen for successful crate training involves taking the puppy to the chosen spot of evacuation immediately following each feeding, whenever it shows signs of readiness to evacuate, and at regular intervals throughout the day. After a feeding and whenever signs are present, the pup must be kept in the spot until it does its business. Every time the pup goes in the appropriate spot, warm and lavish praise must be given. If the pup goes other than in the desired location, it is not its fault but the owner's: young puppies have very limited capacity for holding their excrement, and the owner simply did not provide adequate

Surely these Shar-Pei pups are set in this wire basket for purely photographic reasons. Such a wire enclosure is undoubtedly unsuitable for restricting your pup. Breeder, Bruce Lee Resnick.

opportunity for relief. Through praise for deeds well done and the provision of a clean home quarters, puppies quickly learn the desired location for evacuation. In this way, housebreaking is quickly and thoroughly accomplished with a minimum of correction.

This Bloodhound pup is being kept in a "handyman's dog crate.'"

PAPER TRAINING

When one thinks of housebreaking a dog, one almost inevitably equates it with paper training. Indeed, paper training is one of the oldest and most frequently employed methods of housebreaking; paper training is considered the tried-and-true method and brings with it many merits. Among the advantages of paper training are its simplicity and its well-tried history: paper training seems to come almost instinctually to many new dog owners, and there is no dearth of published material on the paper-training process. Paper training costs very little, and there are no hidden costs either. Essentially all that is required for the paper training procedure is old newspaper; an enclosed, easy-to-clean area in the home; and time and patience. Additionally, paper training demands fewer daily hours of the housebreaking owner's time, as compared with the crate training procedure; and despite the necessary routine required of all housebreaking

methods, paper training is likely the most flexible of them. In view of these advantages, there is little wonder that paper training is the most commonly practiced, and the new dog owner might wish to stop reading right here and begin to paper train his dog. However, the author encourages the reader to read on, for there are a few disadvantages to paper training a dog, and canine behavior experts are becoming more outspoken on these disadvantages and encouraging more and more owners to attempt the crate training method, which is

Paper training has long been the most common method employed for housebreaking the dog. This youngster explains to her Boxer pup what she expects of him.

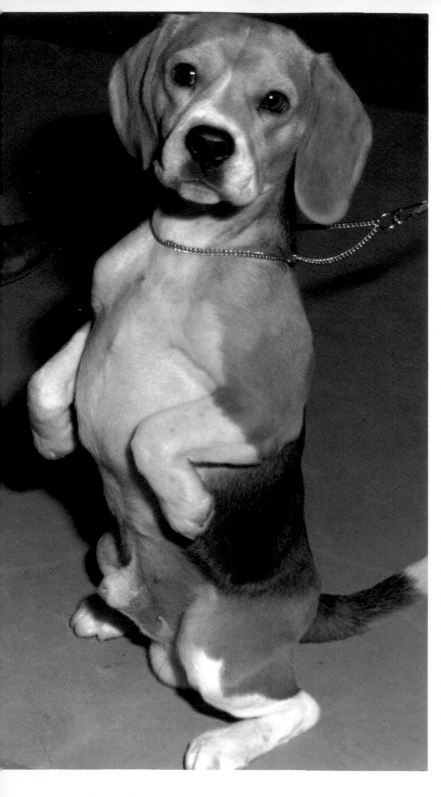

discussed in depth in a separate chapter.

Researchers have found that some dogs, when trained to go on paper in the home, become conditioned to excreting in the home. Such conditioning typically results in one of three training problems. In one case, the dog comes to believe that it is supposed to excrete on papers, and only on papers. Reports document cases in which housebreaking dogs are taken out for a walk after a meal to relieve themselves; with all their will, they retain their excreta for the long duration of the walk; once back in the home (not a moment too soon it seems to them), they race to the paper and finally do their duty, while their bewildered owner looks on. This is a serious problem for the housebreaking owner, for it is very difficult to condition the dog to go outside if paper is continued to be used has a housebreaking tool. One common cause of this situation is excessive praise given when the dog goes on papers and not enough praise when it goes outdoors. Other possible causes include insufficient outings and ill-kept routines. All these three causes are, of course, at the control (and essentially the fault) of the housebreaking owner. There are, however, numerous cases in which dogs become conditioned to going only on papers for no explainable reason other than that the papers are there and the dog is encouraged to go on them. This possible housebreaking problem is for the potential paper trainer to consider.

In a second condition, which is similar to the above described, the dog is conditioned to think that it is O.K. to go in the house as long as it goes on the papers. In this case, the dog in not conditioned to go only on papers, for it freely goes outdoors as well, but is conditioned to go at both locations. To the author, this conditioning is easy to understand: because the dog is praised when it goes on papers, as well as when outdoors, it seems very believable that the dog should come to believe that both are acceptable, if not equally acceptable. The root of this development is likely that the owner did not "wean" the dog off the papers during the later stages of the procedure but continued giving praise throughout the process. Perhaps the greatest danger or setback with this housebreaking development is its usually hidden presence. According to reports, the scenario usually involves an owner's believing that the dog is fully housebroken because it does all its business outdoors. The papers are completely taken away and all is well for a week or so. Then one day, when papers are left on the kitchen (or perhaps worse the living room) floor, the dog excretes, and the puzzled owner is left to wonder why his dog suddenly became "unhousebroken." In such a case, the truth is that the dog was never fully housebroken in the first place, for a housebroken dog is conditioned never to go in the home, under any conditions. The owner is now faced with the problem of conditioning the dog not to use papers, which can be a considerably longer process than housebreaking itself. The owner facing such a problem would probably have done better by employing the crate training method from the start, but then again, as they say, one never knows.

The third problem faced by paper-training housebreakers is the dog's becoming simply conditioned to going in the house. In this case, the dog is not properly conditioned to the papers and associates the praise which occurs in the home when it goes on papers to be simply praise for going in the home. The dog may be conditioned to going outdoors

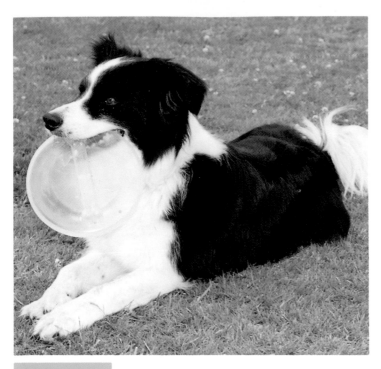

disadvantages as compared to crate training: because paper training relies initially on a somewhat trial-and-error process, correction often becomes more frequently necessary; and, because paper training grants greater flexibility than other housebreaking methods, it can encourage unnecessary slack in the routine, which will inevitably lead to a prolonged housebreaking process.

Paper training is not for everyone, and new dog owners are encouraged to read all the housebreaking discussions in this book before selecting the method for them. It can be said, however, that paper training is often the best housebreaking method for owners who do not have the time or physical ability required for crate training; for owners living in high-rise apartments and condominiums, where making it quickly out the door and down the stairs is an arduous, if not impossible, task; and for owners of small and/or solely indoor dogs which will not be let out regularly in the future.

THE BASICS

Paper training, like all other training methods, relies on consistency, patience, and praise.

Regardless of which housebreaking method is employed, dogs require abundant play and exercise time. The Gumadisc® has proven both safe and effective for this purpose.

as well—but once it is conditioned to believe that going in the home is O.K., the housebreaking owner is faced with a serious problem. The root of the problem is not very clear, nor is it very easy to determine. It is likely that the owner simply did not sufficiently emphasize the rightness of the papers and/or the outdoors, but numerous other causes may also be to blame. Suffice it to say that this problem has been encountered by a number of housebreaking owners, and it is something about which the new dog owner should be aware.

Besides these potential problems, paper training has two

As discussed in the opening chapters, these three concepts are the underlying principles which make successful housebreaking a reality. The housebreaking owner must be consistent with correction and praise, routine and clean-up, and time and effort spent. He must be patient with the dog, allowing it to learn at its own pace, and not becoming disheartened with a slow learner or an occasional mishap. And lastly, the owner must provide warm lavish praise throughout the housebreaking process. Consistency, patience and praise are the primary, indispensable tools with which the paper-training housebreaker has to work, and he is to use them to their utmost value by establishing and maintaining a routine, being tolerant of the dog's wrong doings, and rewarding the dog's successful execution of the trainer's desired tasks. Paper training is based primarily on two sound principles: one, that a dog wants few things more than to please its master; and two, that dogs are essentially clean animals not given to soiling their immediate home or den. By praising the dog for appropriate actions, these actions are reinforced: the dog will come to know what is expected and desired by the owner and will do its utmost to meet the given expectations. Because cleanliness is an already-established quality in the dog, praise (or reinforcement) for actions which keep the environment clean firmly establishes the natural tendency of the dog to become housebroken. In other words, with consistent praise, the dog is quickly brought to the housebroken stage.

This Dachshund pup receives a warm pat on the back for an elimination well done.

THE PROCESS

As with any other housebreaking method, paper training cannot be successful prior to the puppy's third or fourth month of life, as before this time the dog simply does not possess the bodily control necessary to be successfully housebroken. It has been determined that early housebreaking attempts do not prepare the dog for subsequent housebreaking but only hinder and possibly ruin the later attempts at housebreaking.

Paper training begins with the selection of a confined area in which the pup will spend most of its time. This area is lined completely, covering its entire

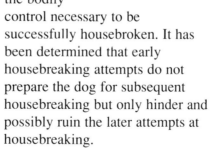

surface, with paper or another suitable medium. (Newspaper is most common simply because it is inexpensive.) There is no best size for the restricted area, but it must be large enough to allow the puppy considerable freedom of movement to play and explore, without being too large to hinder observation or to allow the pup to excrete in a discrete corner. As a rough guideline, the enclosed area for a puppy should be about 6 x 8 feet. Of course, larger pups will require a slightly larger area, while smaller pups will do better in a slightly smaller one. If you do not have this much space available, a smaller space can be provided with good results, but it will be even more important to allow regular outings and walks of considerable duration. An alternative measure, if space is a problem, is the employment of crate training as a housebreaking procedure. Crate training requires less space than paper training, but, like paper training in a smaller area, demands consistent outings and play time.

The mention of additional outings and play for crate-trained and small-area paper-trained dogs is not to suggest that regular outings and play are not a vital part of paper training: paper training is not a substitute for outdoor training for any but solely indoor dogs. The puppy must still be taken out immediately following meals, whenever it shows signs of preparing to relieve itself, and at regular intervals throughout the day. The more often and more regularly the dog is taken out to relieve itself, the more quickly, efficiently, and thoroughly will the housebreaking process be completed. Additionally, insufficient outings may result in a dog that is "houseconditioned" rather than housebroken, as described earlier one of the potential shortcomings of the paper-training procedure.

As mentioned, the restricted area is where the housebreaking dog will spend most of its daily hours. Thus, this area should include the dog's bed, its feeding and water dishes (which should be removed regularly when not in use), a few toys, and a safe chew product—perhaps a Nylabone, Gumabone, or Chooz product. It is important that the area not be cluttered and yet provide enough diversion so that the dog can amuse itself and work off its doggie tensions.

The space requirements of the restricted area will vary somewhat according to the size and activity level of the puppy—of course, all areas will necessarily be larger than a pail, especially for a Rottweiler.

While the pup is in its area, the owner must provide regular observation. Every time the young dog is seen going on the papers, it should be warmly praised while in the action. This is the same form of praise which should be given each and every time the dog goes out of doors. If praise is lavish and consistent, the pup will soon come to realize that going on the paper and going outdoors please its owner, and it will try hard to continue to please him in this manner. This realization typically occurs within the first few days of paper training. When the owner is convinced that the dog is becoming conditioned to the paper-training idea, the paper-covered area should be diminished gradually. It is likely that by this time the dog will have selected a favorite spot at which to excrete, and the papered area should, of course, always recede in this direction, so that the favored spot is the last spot to be removed. It is possible that no such location will be selected by the pup, in which case it is up to the owner's discretion to determine the direction of the paper recession.

Once the papered area diminishes, there will be, of course, an area which is not covered with paper. The housebreaking owner must now encourage the pup to go only on the papered area with the same type of warm praise used earlier. Additionally, if the pup goes other than on the papered area and is caught in the act, then correction, in the form of a brief verbal reprimand, should be given. If the owner does not actually witness the action and follow it immediately with reprimand, then correction is useless and best not given. The dog will not associate the correction with behavior that occurred in the past, and correction in this manner will only serve to confuse and dishearten the dog. Correction should always be given in the form of a brief, sharp verbal reprimand. This author does not believe in physical punishment for any dog, and it has been researched and determined that physical punishment is unnecessary for any form of canine training. Additionally, it has been found that praise, not punishment, is the best motivational factor in canine training. Many well-respected

Looking down upon a portion of this pup's restricted area. Note that the door of the enclosure is left open, telling us that close supervision is underway.

canine behaviorists believe that praise, and praise alone, can train any dog to do any task. An important note with regard to housebreaking is that *no* dog

These Weimaraner pups keep one another company while in the confines of their enclosure.

should *ever* have its nose rubbed in excreta, which was once a common method of housebreaking correction. This is a barbaric practice which serves no purpose other than to denigrate both the owner and his dog. It has been determined that the dog does not understand such action and does not associate it with a wrong doing. A simple firm verbal reprimand is by far the best form of correction.

When the papered area reaches a size of no greater than an opened sheet of newspaper, the dog is nearly housebroken. At this point the housebreaking owner has two options. One is to eliminate the

paper there and then. The other option is to move the papered area closer and closer to the door; when it reaches the door, it can then be eliminated completely, and the owner can determine if the dog is fully housebroken.

If a mishap happens at this time, it should occur at or near the respective door; this will necessitate correction, and the papered area should be re-established at the door; after a day, the owner should again try to eliminate the paper, watch carefully for signs that the dog is to go, and let the dog out immediately. The next couple of days will require close watching, but shortly you should have a completely housebroken dog.

If the accident occurs some distance from the door, however, then the dog is not yet ready to be completely housebroken and should be maintained in a restricted, small papered area. The owner should make every effort to watch the dog carefully and adjust its behavior accordingly. The papered area can then again be removed when the owner feels that the dog has finally got it. Again, close supervision will be required for the first few days after the papered area has been eliminated.

LITTERBOX TRAINING

Litterbox training differs from crate training and paper training in that, with litterbox training, the dog will be conditioned to know that eliminating in the house is O.K., provided that the excrement is in the box. Litterbox training does not necessarily mean that a "litterbox" will be the housebreaking object, for a dog may be housetrained to go at a specific location in the garage, on newspapers, etc., and, in the context of this book, it would still be considered litterbox training. Thus, as a definition, litterbox training is a housebreaking method which conditions the dog to excrete in an appropriate location in the home, regardless of whether it is on newspapers, or in an actual litterbox. Within this definition, there are two possible goals in litterbox

training: one, the dog is conditioned to go both outdoors and in the litterbox; or two, the dog is conditioned to go only in the litterbox. In the former, the praise and correction will be roughly the same as for paper training: the dog will be praised when it goes on the papered area and when it goes outdoors; however, unlike paper training, the praise for going indoors will not diminish as the process wears on but will continue to be on par with the praise received for going outdoors. To achieve the latter goal, a solely indoor-going dog, praise is given only when the dog goes in the appropriate place indoors. Of course, many litterbox-trained dogs are never to see the outdoors, and thus such conditioning becomes academic. For those dogs who will experience both the home and the wood, however, solely litterbox training requires special correction and praise.

The reader may wonder why an owner would want his dog to go only indoors, even if the animal is to be taken out. The reason why, for most owners who desire a solely indoor-going dog, is the owner's preference not to have to pooper-scoop-and-plastic-bag after his dog—pooper-scooper laws are extending well beyond the city these days. Even in areas where there are not pooper-scooper laws, owners may desire a solely indoor-going dog because they do not wish the well-groomed or child-occupied yard to be soiled with dog feces. In all these cases, and in any other instance in which the owner desires a dog to go only indoors, litterbox training is the method of choice.

Litterbox training follows roughly the same procedure as paper training, and the owner who is considering litterbox training is encouraged to read carefully the chapter dealing with paper training, as the

same restrictions and possible problems which apply to paper training also apply to litterbox training. Additionally, the litterbox-training owner must consider the instinctive scent-marking role which the dog's waste plays.

Dogs use their urine and feces as a primary mode of social communication with other dogs. The dog's excrement is a unique signature—not unlike our thumb prints—which identifies the dog to all other dogs, and many other animals as well. Because scent marking plays a very significant part in the social development and interaction of dogs, it would be unwise to eliminate entirely any dog's scent marking (this, of course, does not apply to solely indoor dogs, who need only to eliminate in their box, and dogs who will be conditioned to go both indoors and outdoors). Therefore, for the indoor–outdoor dog which is to be litterbox trained, it is best that the owner allow the dog to urinate outdoors, while keeping fecal excretion to the litterbox.

THE SOLELY INDOOR DOG

Like all other housebreaking methods, litterbox training cannot be started before the pup reaches three to four months of age, as before this time the dog simply does not possess the bladder and bowel control necessary to be successfully housebroken.

To start litterbox training, select an area that has an easy-to-clean floor surface and is free from hazards, excessive distractions, and hard-to-reach places. Preferably, this is the area where

All members of the family, including small children, must be aware of the rules and restrictions regarding the canine pet—and abide by them.

the litterbox will be located indefinitely, as it is always best not to move it until after the housebreaking process is completed, for then there is a greater chance that the dog will not become too confused.

As in the paper-training method, the enclosed housebreaking area should initially be completely lined with papers, covering the entire floor surface. The entire enclosed area must be large enough to allow the puppy considerable freedom of movement to play and explore. As a rough guideline, the enclosed area for a small or toy dog should be about 4 x 6 feet. Of course, larger puppies will require a larger area, perhaps 6 x 8. If you do not have this much space available, a

40

smaller space can be provided with good results, but it will be even more important to allow free play time of considerable duration. As an additional note, the author believes that few other than the toy breeds, some of the small terriers, and few other dogs are physically or mentally suited for solely indoor existence.

Once the area is determined and covered, the litterbox should be placed within it; the litterbox should be lined with the same medium which covers the floor, which most always is newspaper. The owner can then add the dog's bed, its feeding and water dishes (which should be removed regularly when not in use), a few toys, and a safe chew product—perhaps a Nylabone, Gumabone, or Chooz product. It is important that the area not be cluttered and yet provide enough diversion so that the dog can amuse itself and work off its doggie tensions.

While the pup is in its area, the owner must provide regular observation. The dog should be praised every time it goes on the papers—which is every time it goes for the first day to two, as the area is completely lined with papers. This praise will condition the dog to associate a pleasurable experience with its excretion; the dog will soon realize that going on the paper pleases its owner and will try hard to continue to please him in this manner. This realization typically occurs within the first few days of training. When the owner feels sure that the dog is becoming conditioned to the idea, the paper-covered area should be reduced, thus leaving a patch of bare floor. This bare flooring is to serve as the first no-no within the enclosed area. Soon this no-no area will include all of the area except the litterbox, thus leaving the dog to determine that the box is the only appropriate place to excrete.

It is likely that, by the time the papered area begins to recede, the dog will have selected a favorite spot at which to excrete, and the litterbox should, of course, be placed at that spot. It is possible that no such location will be selected by the pup, in which case the litterbox can remain where it is and the papered area recede in the direction determined at the owner's discretion.

Now that there is a bare area of the floor, the housebreaking owner must encourage the pup to go only on the papered area, ideally in the litterbox, with the same type of warm praise used earlier. Additionally, if the pup goes other than on the papered area and is caught in the act, then correction, in the form of a brief verbal reprimand, should be given. If the owner does not actually witness the action and follow it

"If the owner does not actually witness the action and follow it immediately with reprimand, then correction is useless and best not given."

immediately with reprimand, then correction is useless and best not given. The dog will not associate the correction with behavior which occurred in the past, and correction in this manner will only serve to confuse and dishearten the dog. Correction should always be given in the form of a brief, sharp verbal reprimand. This author does

not believe in physical punishment for any dog, and it has been researched and determined that physical punishment is unnecessary for any form of canine training.

The papered area should continue to diminish gradually in the direction of the litterbox; as the papered area becomes smaller and smaller, it may be necessary to increase observation time if it seems that the dog is not quite

grasping the owner's intention. As with the paper-trained dog, who is praised more strongly for going out of doors than for going on the paper, the litterbox-trained dog should be praised with special lavishness and warmth when it goes in the litterbox. At the same time, as the process continues, praise should be lessened for the dog's going on the paper outside the box. With appropriate use of praise, the puppy should have a clear idea has to the owner's intentions by the close of the housebreaking process, when the dog goes only in the litterbox for several straight days.

THE INDOOR–OUTDOOR DOG

The owner of the indoor–outdoor dog faces the special consideration mentioned earlier in this chapter, namely the fact that the dog's elimination serves the primary function of social communication. This communication is especially prevalent in unneutered male dogs. Owners need to be aware that urination, and to some degree defecation, serve the strong canine communication instinct. Canine behaviorists have determined that this instinct is strong in both sexes, though apparently more so in the male animal. Canine behaviorists also believe that urination likely serves a greater role in this social communication behavior than defecation, if for no other reason than that urination is the more frequent and more easily enacted of the two scent markings. Based on these findings and beliefs, the author feels that the indoor–outdoor dog should be trained only to retain its feces, and that it should be free to scent mark its outdoor environment as would any other dog. If the dog is free to scent mark with urine—believably the more important of the two types of scent marking—then the trainer/owner is not faced with the difficult task of purging the dog of one of its deeply rooted drives; rather, this drive is merely adapted and modified to meet the needs of both owner and dog. In the end, it seems that such training would result in a happier canine companion than a training method which strove to produce a dog that never scent marked in the outdoors, though it experienced such an environment on a regular basis.

As with all the other housebreaking methods presented in this book, litterbox training for the indoor–outdoor dog is best suited to a specific type of dog owner. According to reports, most dog owners who opt for this method of training are owners of medium- to large-sized dogs who live in urban areas. These are the owners who most likely are affected by pooper-scooper laws and owners who feel the glare of neighbors each time their Bullmastiff squats at the curb— regardless of whether they clean up immediately after or not. The second most common owner who opts for this method of housebreaking is the suburban dog owner who keeps proper care of his lawn and garden, who likes his dog to roam freely about the yard but who prefers that the dog not soil the landscaping. Also, like all other housebreaking methods described in this book, litterbox training for the outdoor dog has its special demands, which may or may not be within the realm of time and commitment available to the interested owner. But, if the owner is willing to make the effort, this method has its definte rewards.

Puppies experience great and rapid changes during their first year of life. Owners must consider these changes and their effects in order to cultivate a healthy person-to-pet relationship. German Shepherd Dog.

43

THE PROCESS

Of course, this housebreaking method cannot be started until after the dog attains control of its excretory system, sometime after it is three months of age. For all intents and purposes, this type of litterbox training is identical to the aforementioned training method for the solely indoor dog, with the exception that in this training the dog will be taken out for walks and playtime, and special training and scheduling will be required when so doing. Before proceeding, the reader is encouraged to read the previous section for the indoor dog, if he has not yet done so.

Walks and play time need to be carefully incorporated into the housebreaking routine; they should be timed initially so that they occur at times when the dog is least likely to defecate. In this case, walks and outdoor play should occur just after indoor defecation and/or prior to feeding. If given the choice between the two times, select the former, for it has two advantages: by taking the dog out, which almost inevitably is a pleasurable experience, the owner can use it as a reward for correct behavior, and secondly, shortly after the pup has had a complete bowel movement is the least likely time that it will defecate.

While outdoors, the same rules of correction and praise for appropriate behavior apply as they do for indoor behavior. In this type of litterbox training, the dog should receive a brief verbal reprimand when the owner catches it defecating outdoors; contrarily, when the dog defecates at the appropriate location indoors it should receive warm, lavish praise. Urination is a different matter, if the trainer heeds the word of caution given by the author, for urination outdoors should pass unnoticed, while indoor urination should be proper. With urination, the dog should be allowed to urinate outdoors, thus satisfying its innate instinct of social scent communication, but should be praised for urinating at the appropriate place indoors.

Because outdoor excretion is second nature to dogs, it is necessary that the owner provide acute observation of the dog while it is taken out during the entire housebreaking procedure. If a lax owner allows his dog to defecate unnoticed in the outdoors, training the dog to be a solely indoor reliever may become a nearly impossible task. A special difficulty for the owner who employs this training procedure is the fact that detection of an "accident" is virtually impossible unless the only outdoors that the dog experiences is an enclosed yard free of other dogs.

As can be seen, litterbox

training the indoor–outdoor dog is demanding, for supervision is required for the indoor training, and the housebreaking owner must also provide a very considerable amount of outdoor time and acute observation. This is not to discourage the reader, however, for in the end, this housebreaking method is as likely to generate the desired results as any of the other housebreaking methods, provided it is approached with forethought and consideration and is executed with the same patience, persistence, and praise required of all housebreaking routines.

These Akita pups were born in Norway. The black pup is a male, and the white one is a female. While some people claim that females are easier to housebreak, such generalizations are really not accurate.

45

MISHAPS AND MISTAKES

Mishaps and mistakes seem to happen inevitably in almost every housebreaking process, especially

in the case of first-time owners. By far, the most common cause of a mishap is the owner's rushing the dog to complete housebrokeness: either the owner stops the housebreaking conditioning too soon or the housebreaking process is gone through too quickly, without the necessary thoroughness required of all housebreaking procedures. If the mishap occurs within a week or two after housebreaking has been "completed," then the owner has no alternative but to revert to the earlier housebreaking situation.

If a mishap occurs while the housebreaking process is still ongoing, there is a good chance that the dog was not given adequate opportunity to relieve itself in the appropriate place. It may be the case of a changed diet, which the owner did not calculate into the observation or outing schedule, or it may simply be that the owner was away too long or too occupied to perceive correctly the dog's need. If a mishap occurs during the housebreaking process, it is almost always the fault of the housebreaking owner, who should remember this fact and adjust his anger, frustration, and correction accordingly. Mishaps during the housebreaking process can set the entire procedure back, but this is usually the case only when the mishaps are several in number; in other words, a single mishap is not to be fretted. The rule of correction, namely correct only the behavior that is witnessed, applies to all mishaps, at all stages of the housebreaking and post-housebreaking process.

dog, once fully housebroken, should ever become unhousebroken. It may be necessary, in the case of a sick dog, to provide the animal with a papered area or free access to the outdoors, but under no condition (except in the case of a paralyzed or mortally ill animal) should the

A delightful litter of Boxer pups. Breeder, Rick Tomita.

Mishaps and mistakes that occur long after the housebreaking procedure is finished are usually the result of sickness, especially sickness that affects the digestive system. If a dog soils the home after it is surely housebroken, it is a relatively sure sign that the dog is suffering from an ill condition; of course, the dog should receive prompt veterinary attention. No

animal need to soil its home. The common belief that dogs will soil their environment out of spite, or for other reasons, is simply not true. Dogs which are not sick but which soil their home, regardless of the age of the dog, are simply not housebroken and need to experience (or re-experience) the housebreaking procedure. Puppies which "refuse" or cannot be housebroken are usually too young to be housebroken. It is important to remember that all dogs mature at their own individual pace, which can even differ from that of littermates. If the dog is under six, or even seven, months of age and refuses to be housebroken, it is likely that the dog is simply too young. Dogs over the age of six or seven months which cannot be housebroken typically have either a disease, a physical malformation, or a behavioral problem. If your dog or puppy cannot be housebroken, it is wise to have a veterinarian check the dog. Report all possible symptoms to the veterinarian. Additionally, bring a stool sample and, if requested, a urine sample, as these will assist in any diagnosis.

Of course, a puppy which takes longer than expected to become fully housebroken is not necessarily an impossible dog to housebreak: dogs, like humans, are each individuals, learning and conforming at their own pace. If the owner has chronic difficulty housebreaking his dog, professional trainers can likely come to his assistance.

Many puppies, even puppies as obviously well-bred as these Shar-Pei, develop a case of worms during their first few weeks of life. It is of utmost importance that puppies be checked for these parasites and treated by a veterinarian during the high-risk time.

FEEDING AND HOUSEBREAKING

Feeding and housebreaking are inseparably related: all is for naught in the housebreaking process if the puppy's food and feeding schedule are not considered in the housebreaking routine. The simple reason for this is that the puppy's rapid digestion and limited capacity to retain its excrement mean that housebreaking outings will necessarily be timed with feeding and watering if the housebreaking procedure is to succeed. As mentioned earlier, puppies around the age of six months have the capacity to retain their excrement for about four hours, which can be lengthened to about eight hours during the night hours with careful planning. These four- and eight-hour times refer, of course, to the dog who has had his meal and then has been allowed to relieve itself. Additionally, these four- and eight-hour holding capacities are in no way constants, for they can vary considerably

from pup to pup and are reliant upon many variables.

Under normal circumstances, the pressure exerted on the excretory system by a full stomach causes the need of the puppy to relieve itself between 15 to 30 minutes after the meal. This is the crucial time in all housebreaking processes; it is a time when close observation and/or outings are requisite. After elimination of the bowels and bladder, it is a matter of time before the digestive system can complete its task and prepare additional material for excretion; it is this matter of time which allows for the roughly four-hour holding capacity. What is meant by "normal circumstances" is a condition in which the puppy is fed a sound diet that is consistent with the one to which it is accustomed. The digestive system of the puppy is very sensitive to change, and it is important for the new owner to feed with great consistency regarding the nutriment and contents of the daily foodstuff.

Regarding the specific diet to feed the pup, it is best, if not essential, that the dog be fed the same foods (same brand name and all) which the breeder or pet shop fed to the pup. The puppy should be fed the same exact foods, in the same quantities, at the same times, for a least the first few days, until the puppy is given time to settle into its new home environment. Feeding in this way will not only help to prevent digestive upsets but will also be a source of comfort to the canine creature of habit. If you are not provided with the puppy's diet and feeding schedule as a matter of course in the sale of the dog, by all means ask the seller and he will gladly pass it on to you.

Made from digestible cheese protein, this Chooz treat is purported to be the most healthy dog chew available. If it's too hard for your dog, simply microwave it for a minute or so and it becomes a crispy, crunchy delectable dog biscuit. It comes in many sizes.

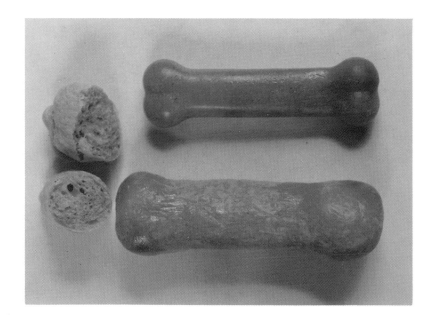

Of course, changing the diet is necessary, and after about five days in the new home, the puppy can be changed gradually to a new diet by adding small quantities of new food to its staple diet. As a rough example, consider the ten-week puppy who is eating one cup of moistened dry food three times a day. The owner should begin changing the pup's diet by reducing the staple ration by one tablespoon and adding one tablespoon of the new food for the first and second day's meals. On the third day, the owner should reduce the old staple ration by an additional tablespoon, adding another tablespoon of the new food. The third day's ration should also be fed on the fourth day. This process can be continued until the puppy is completely weaned from the old food and is eating only the new. It is important during this time to observe the dog's bowel movements. Loose stools and straining during bowel movements can signal too rapid a change in diet or a diet insufficient for the puppy's needs. In these cases, revert to the previous ration in which more of the old staple was included—or adapt the diet to provide for the dog's needs. When

stools return to normal, begin again changing the diet—keeping in mind any adaptations that may have been necessary. Should the adverse condition be prolonged, contact the veterinarian. Because of the possible negative reactions which a dog can have to a change in diet, it is best that such changes not coincide with the housebreaking process: if the dog is to be weaned from puppy to semi-moist kibble, do so before you commence housebreaking.

Keeping meal time constant and changing it only gradually from the schedule which was established by the breeder is as important as the consistency of meal content in the early days of new dog ownership. Meals should be provided according to a regular, strict schedule, again following the one the breeder established and pet shop followed. As with food content, this schedule should be

A boy and his puppy enjoying quality time together on the summer lawn. Proper feeding contributes greatly to canine health and happiness.

51

closely followed for the first few days of ownership, until the puppy settles into its new home. Changing the feeding schedule, which may or may not be desired, must also follow along lines similar to the changing of the meal content. Should the schedule be altered, it should be so adjusted in no greater than half-hour increments, every other day, until the desired time is reached. As when changing the content, the

owner must provide close observation during the schedule-changing process: even though it is primarily the pressure exerted by a full stomach that generates the need to evacuate, it is possible that the puppy's body clock will stimulate excretion in accordance with a previously established schedule. Because of this possibility, as well as possible adjustment problems due to the

change in routine, it is best that the housebreaking owner make all feeding schedule adjustments before the housebreaking process is started or after it is completed.

Based on the constancy required by the puppy of its food and feeding schedule, the new owner can clearly see the importance of accustoming the new dog to the desired foods and schedule prior to the start of the housebreaking process. Such accustoming requires foresight and planning. The new owner should thus draw up a proposed house-breaking schedule which will work in light of the owner's work and social schedule. Feeding times should then be adjusted to concur with the owner's available time for close observation, walks, and other necessary housebreaking efforts. The puppy should be fully adjusted to the given schedule for at least a full week prior to the start of the housebreaking routine. This planning and scheduling, while important and very useful to

52

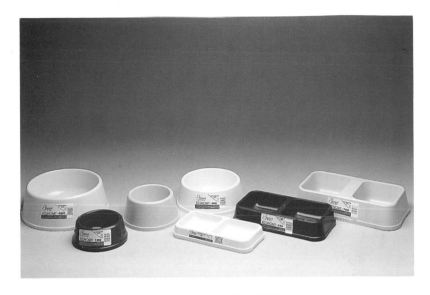

quick and successful housebreaking, is not absolutely necessary, however. If a conflict arises for any reason, and the puppy's feeding schedule needs adjustment, provided that the adjustment is not too severe, the housebreaking process should be continued while the dog's schedule is being changed. Of course, in these situations, the owner will have to consider the possible consequences and realize that the entire housebreaking process may be temporarily slowed a bit. But, in the opinion of the author, it is better to continue the housebreaking process, if possible, while making the change, then to stop the process short and have to begin anew, which can lead to considerable confusion of the young dog. Thus we can see the importance of planning.

WATER

Water should be provided to the housebroken dog at all times. For the young puppy, water is best provided at regularly scheduled times—at least six times a day, and certainly after each meal. At each watering time, the pup should be allowed to drink to its full, and then, of course, taken out to relieve itself. Water should never be refused to a thirsty pup, but water constantly provided will inhibit the housebreaking process unless constant supervision is available. Not all dogs have the same basic water requirements. Large dogs are better able to store water and can therefore go longer periods without a drink, if necessary. Small dogs and puppies typically have less ability to store water, requiring that they frequently have water available.

TRAINING

For most dog owners, there is nothing more dreaded than an incorrigible dog, and yet in most cases of canine incorrigibility, the fault lies in a lack of early training and conditioning by the owner. While still in puppyhood, all dogs should be taught the four basic commands come, sit, lie, and down. Additionally, all young dogs should become well conditioned to basic lead training.

Basic training is requisite for all dogs, regardless of the breed. American Pit Bull Terrier owned by Mike and Terry Walsh.

The basic training techniques described in this chapter in no way interfere with the housebreaking routine. As a matter of fact, training such as the sit and stay commands can be included as an important part of the necessary quality time which an owner must spend with his dog during the housebreaking process. The training methods described here are all basic, and some can begin even before housebreaking is started.

Early training and conditioning are crucially important to the dog's future socialization and advanced learning. They bring the owner and young dog close together at an early age through quality interaction, challenge, and accomplishment. The four basic commands are easy to teach and are within the learning ability of every

healthy dog. These four commands, combined with proper lead conditioning, form the basis for advanced training and obedience, and, even of themselves, commands and lead conditioning help shape the dog's behavior to socially acceptable, managcable behavior.

The trainer of young dogs must remember that the puppy's attention span is very short. Each training session should be kept to no more than a 15-minute duration, and should occur at least on a daily basis. For best results, training sessions will be short and will occur several times daily. It has been found beyond a doubt that young dogs respond best and quickest to short, frequent training sessions.

COME

The come and the sit commands are possibly the easiest of all to teach and are often the first commands the puppy learns. The owner should begin conditioning the puppy to the come command the first day

home. Each time the pup's food dish is placed on the floor, the trainer should state clearly, in an authoritative tone, "Come." This should be stated each and every time the dog is given a treat, a toy, or its mcal. Later, when walks on a lead become part of the daily routine, the come command should be given each time the owner takes the lead from its place of keeping. In general, state "Come" every time something pleasing is given to the pup which he must come to receive. The pup's natural curiosity, hunger, or desire for a walk will inevitably bring the puppy prancing. By hearing the come command often and associating it with pleasing

Never question the determination and abilities of the canine. Born to track, this Bloodhound gets a good workout while honing his obedience and agility skills. Owner, Celeste Meade.

55

rewards, the puppy will quickly master the come command. The polishing stages involve providing the dog with distractions, such as other people, dogs, or play things, and commanding the dog to come. When it does, warm, lavish praise and possibly a treat (especially helpful in the early stages) should be given as reward: the dog must be let to know that it did good by coming. If distractions are too much at first, the dog is not yet conditioned enough to the command. Continue, perhaps with more frequency, the primary conditioning phases. Many puppies learn the come command even before they begin the housebreaking process (four

months). Typically, the come command takes two to three weeks of regular daily conditioning to be fully mastered by the dog.

SIT

The sit command is similarly easy to teach, and it too can begin on the pup's first day home. What makes teaching this command easy is the construction of the dog's neck and spine, which makes it difficult for the dog to look upward from a standing position. To condition the dog to the sit command, begin by holding objects that are appealing to the dog in a raised hand. When the standing dog notices the object, give the sit command in an authoritative tone as the dog sits to attain a better, more comfortable view. As soon as the dog sits, extend plenteous praise. In the case of teaching the sit command, because sitting is so natural a habit for the dog, it may take longer for the dog to associate the command with the action, and thus fully learn or master the training. However, consistency will always pay off: the dog will soon associate the command with the action, and in turn the action with the pleasing reward. In the end you will have a dog who knows the sit command.

After the come command is mastered, the come and sit commands can be performed in

Once your dog has become adjusted to using a regular leash, try walking with a retractable one. These clever devices give your dog more freedom when in an open area or field. Photo courtesy of Rolf C. Hagen Corp.

conjunction with each other. The puppy can be called at meal time (the come command) and, before the meal is placed down, made to sit by your holding the food dish high in the hand and commanding "Sit." Thus the meal can serve as dual reward for both come and sit training. Of course, meal time is not the only time that the come and sit commands can be taught collectively, for they can be executed using any reward, including a toy, a treat, or simple praise. Praise, warm and lavish, is one of dog's favorite rewards.

LIE

The lie command is similar to the sit command, except that the puppy does not lie to see things better but rather to relax and retire. Teaching the lie command involves plenty of good observation. As is the case with sitting, lying is a natural action, and it may take the dog a few weeks of consistently hearing the command in conjunction with his action to begin to associate the command with the action and understand what behavior is desired by the owner. To teach the lie command, observe the pup carefully. Whenever the pup begins to lie down, state "Lie" in a firm voice. As soon as the dog lies, give him warm praise. It is best to say simply "Lie" and not "Lie down," for when the down

English Springer
Spaniel parent and
offspring owned by
Berger and Roth.

command is taught some confusion may result. Once you think the puppy understands the command, you can test his learning by giving the command when the pup shows no signs of lying down. At first it is best not to have distractions present, but as the command becomes more firmly implanted, distractions should be presented to increase the training. As with all other training procedures, successful compliance by the dog deserves immediate reward.

DOWN

The down command is certainly more difficult to teach the puppy than the first three more-basic commands. Nonetheless, the down command is an essential one for the puppy to learn. Unlike the previous three commands, in which the owner was using the natural behavior of the puppy to facilitate training, the down command involves breaking the puppy of an almost instinctive habit.

Several different methods are proposed by various authorities on canine training. Some involve more force and punishment, while others rely on quick reflexes and praise. Because the author believes that observation and praise can train any dog, the latter of type training is presented. Teaching the down command can be very easy if the puppy is never rewarded for jumping up. It may sound too simple, but in too many cases do owners condone undesirable behavior because it seems cute of a puppy. Stopping a dog from jumping, after it was allowed to jump as a puppy, is exceedingly more difficult than conditioning a puppy not to jump from the time it enters the new home.

The key to teaching the down command then is not allowing the puppy up in the first place. When the puppy comes to greet you or to play, watch closely that it stops in front of you and makes no motion to jump on you. If the pup makes motion to jump, time its jump with a quick step backwards. The pup will have nothing to plant on and will return to the standing position. Give the down command quickly and sharply as the pup "falls" back to the standing position. As soon as the puppy is in the position, give warm praise. All members of the household, as well as frequent guests, should be informed of this procedure and follow it. If just one person allows the pup to jump, then the training process can be made considerably more difficult.

Jumping on furniture requires a little more "hands-on" training. Watch the puppy. As soon as it jumps on the furniture, take its forepaws—or the entire puppy if it is completely atop the furniture— and return them (or it) swiftly to

"Teaching the down command can be very easy if the puppy is never rewarded for jumping up."

This Beagle is wearing a training collar, also known as a choke collar. The purpose of this type of collar is, of course, not to choke the dog but to assist in lead training.

possible, thus allowing the attachment of a name tag, vaccination tag, and license. The best collar for a puppy is made of either soft leather or nylon. It should fit comfortably around the neck, not too loose to be pulled over the head, nor too tight that it will pinch the skin. The puppy may struggle and strain a bit, maybe even whimper, when the collar is first put on. Soon, however, he will adjust fine. In a day or two, the puppy will not even realize that a collar is around its neck.

After the pup is well acclimated to the feel of the collar, try attaching a lead to it. Allow the pup to run around freely with the collar dragging behind. Let the pup sniff, bite and paw at the lead, thus coming to know it as a harmless object. These lead-acclimating periods should be done a few times a day for two to three days before actual lead

the ground while commanding "Down" in a clear, sharp voice. As soon as the puppy is returned to the floor, give lavish praise. Again, all members of the household should be informed of this practice. Whenever observation is not possible, the puppy should be kept in its chosen play area or crate, where there is not furniture on which to jump.

LEAD TRAINING

All puppies should become accustomed to the collar and lead at an early age, eight to ten weeks. The collar comes first and should be put on the puppy as soon as training begins in earnest.

Lead training commences with the puppy's first walk on the lead. Some experts believe that the first walks should actually be taken in the home, the area with which the pup is most familiar. The author sees merit in the idea but believes that such is not necessary. During the first few walks, allow the pup to lead you. Apply gentle but firm restraint and never pull or jerk the puppy. After a few walks, the puppy will learn and appreciate the restrictions of the lead.

The first lead-training lesson involves teaching the puppy to heel. Before beginning this and other lead training lessons, it is usually best that the pup has mastered the aforementioned basic commands, such as come, sit, and stay. Lead training is not only more difficult for the pup but often uses these basic commands during the lessons.

Begin the heel lesson with the pup sitting on your left side, collar and lead attached. Hold the end of the lead in your right hand and the middle of the lead in your left hand, forming a visual J-loop. Release the lead from your left hand for a moment and place it, palm facing the puppy, in front of the puppy's nose. When ready, raise your left hand and firmly give the command "Heel" while beginning the walk with your left foot first. As you step, return your left hand to the lead, again forming the desired J-loop. For the first few (even many) lead training lessons the pup will inevitably attempt to

The Airedale Terrier stands among the most able and adaptable of canines. Here Holly performs for owners and friends at Jackson Kennels.

prance in front of you or fall back behind you. However, the object of training to heel is to keep the dog walking even with your left side. Therefore, when the pup lunges forward, give a quick, sharp tug at the lead while commanding "Heel." The tug is not to lift the pup into the air or cause pain but simply to bring the pup to associate discomfort with lunging in front during a walk. As soon as the pup is brought back to the side of the walker, praise and reward (verbal and/or other) should be given. The key to teaching the heel lesson is persistence, consistency, and praise. Do not get

As a companion, there's no beating a well-trained dog. Bouvier des Flandres owned by Van Vliet Kennels.

disheartened after six or even 12 unsuccessful lessons. Keep the lessons short, about 15 minutes at most, and perform them several times a day, three to four being ideal. Many pups take several weeks of such training, but the end result is well worth the effort: the heel command is the most basic lead-training command and the command upon which all future lead training is built.

SUMMING IT UP

The lessons and commands just covered in this chapter are the basic training which every puppy should have. A puppy untrained in these basics can become both a nuisance and a hazard as a dog. Additionally, the author encourages all dog owners to seek additional obedience training after their dog reaches six or so months of age. Obedience classes are best attended by both owner and dog and assist greatly in solidifying the human-to-pet bond. Additionally, it should be mentioned that the above-described training methods reflect but one of many different styles of puppy training. While the author believes that these reflect the best school of thought regarding puppy training, all owners who find difficulty training their dog this way are encouraged to seek other training methods.

Two six-week-old Old English Sheepdog puppies owned by John and Danna Bankovskis.

INDEX